Unapologetically Dope

Unapologetically Dope

Lessons for Black Women and Girls on Surviving and Thriving in the Tech Field

A. Nicki Washington, Ph.D.

This book is dedicated to every Black woman and girl who has ever been told they're "too" anything: mean, angry, loud, arrogant, unattractive, strong, weak, rude, skinny, fat, confident, ambitious, educated, opinionated, assertive, emotional, dramatic, bossy, independent, and Black. You are everything. Flourish. Unapologetically.

Unapologetic (*adjective*)-not acknowledging or expressing regret.

Dope (*adjective*)-extremely good.

Contents

Foreword

I wish I had had this book when I was a young STEM undergraduate, or for that matter, anywhere along my winding road as a technologist-turned activist/educator. For generations, Black women technologists (myself included) have learned through the school of hard knocks the critical wisdoms that weren't written so completely anywhere. It is rare for that knowledge to be addressed to us, written down for us to read over and again. This book was written so that we might find that wisdom here. Finding it for me, at this time, spoke to me in a way that was unexpected and so very powerful.

The strong truths that so many young Black women technologists and educators of them need to hear are now succinctly encapsulated in the book you have in your hands. I know from my own firsthand experiences as a Black woman in a technical world the lack of understanding and sensitivity that exists towards women like us. So many (from the powerful tech giants, to everyday coworkers, underlings, and even our students) overlook our intellectual investment and the sweat and blood we shed in order to do innovative, life-changing work that contributes to the greater good, all while often being underpaid as we work to "be twice as good to get half as much."

And about that. Never has someone so adeptly connected the blessing and curse of the engrained "twice as good to get half as much" mantra that we are taught from childhood than Dr. Washington. Her work reminds me of how we often fail to actually win because we're working so hard to be better than our peers, to be perfect. Perfect that doesn't ask for help. Better that exists to serve others, conditioned to be the "fixer." But better often doesn't allow for the risk taking that defines successful entrepreneurs. As she shares, we often see others succeed with ideas we had years before because we were too busy trying to be perfect to take a chance on a new idea, not to mention the ones that get outright stolen. Young women (and not-so-young ones too!): Please heed this stumbling block! We need the products and services that are born out of ideas that only you can perfect, but you must be willing to allow yourselves a break from being perfect to see your ideas through to fruition.

This books speaks to the Black woman. Nicki takes you by the collar and plays the role of square shooter, a person she refers to as one of the people you must have in your life, your tribe, who will just tell you like it is. She tells you what you should do (stay current, know your adversaries, etc.), what you shouldn't do (get comfortable, ignore your physical and mental health, and more), and addresses those familiar demons, chief of which can be imposter syndrome, particularly sinister to Black female computer scientists in a field in which we're rarely pictured as the ideal contributor. Her own experience of soldiering on, even as her father fought for his life, brought me to tears and reminded me that I am not alone in my journey either. I relate (as so many of us can) through my own experience of losing my husband to disease, while simultaneously raising four young children and working to launch five schools that would be chief in the foundation of the Computer Science for All movement (which I later founded and led in Chicago Public Schools). I've seen this type of unsung dedication amongst us time and again, which is why I join with Dr. Nicki and ask you to say out loud, "We Are Dope!" We are dedicated, tenacious, and the very definition of grit. No apologies necessary. You will thank Dr. Nicki for reminding you of this, as our modesty often helps us deny it. Balance some of that humility we have been so well conditioned to exhibit with the knowledge that you are a unique and necessary contributor to tech and therefore to our global way of life.

I am grateful that Dr. Nicki took the time to share from her deep and abiding experiences as a thrice-degreed computer scientist/educator (she knows of what she speaks y'all!) to become part of your tribe of folks that you need to keep you on your path. As I reflect on all the roles I have had in my career, from technologist, to entrepreneur, educator, and now CEO of a non-profit dedicated to intersectional gender and pay equity for all tech women, I realize that we all need the wisdom of someone who looks like us who has walked the path we're on to bring clarity of purpose to our situations where the lack thereof can dislodge us from our way.

So here's what I think will happen. You'll find yourself in these pages. Some things you see in this mirror you'll like, others will give you pause. Both will be for your good. But most importantly, relish this gift and return to it over and again and realize that you are the dope folks the world needs. We need your ideas. We need your solutions. We need your contributions. We need your attention to the datasets and the algorithms now silently in place leaving out or, worse, harming a world of folk you definitely would not. And don't forget to take care of you, to appreciate yourself, and more than perhaps you ever realized the need to, lift up and appreciate the dope in your sisters alike! Dr. Nicki just lightened our load. So pass it on.

Enjoy the feast!

Brenda Darden Wilkerson
CEO and President, AnitaB.org

Introduction

This book is so long overdue and necessary. I'm still unsure how or why I thought something like this was already available. Nevertheless, Muva to the rescue! To every Black woman and girl reading this, we've been waiting for you!

I always wanted to write something like this because I was already providing this advice and encouragement to women and girls I spoke to, be it at conferences, workshops, or in casual conversation. However, I would place it on the back burner to work on something else, assuming that someone else would accept the challenge. Then I was invited several months ago to moderate a panel as part of the kickoff for the inaugural blackcomputeHER Fellows program. I spent the entire day listening in amazement as approximately 20 Black women in graduate school and early careers discussed their interests and goals. I was simultaneously inspired and startled. There were so many dope women in one room doing amazing things in computing! However, many of their concerns and challenges (many of which weren't computing related) sounded so familiar to those I had as an undergraduate, graduate student, and professional.

It was in that moment that I realized it was time. The more things changed, the more they stayed the same. Being Black and a woman in this country is already stressful enough, given the current times we live in. It can be even more challenging when navigating (or integrating) a department or organization where you're one of the few, if not the only one who looks like you. *This* book and *this* advice were needed, now more than ever.

According to the most recent Taulbee Survey, only 1% of all computing-related bachelor's degrees are awarded to Black women. Couple this with the lack of diversity and inclusion efforts in Silicon Valley and we have the problem we're facing: a lack of diverse and qualified talent in a field with more jobs than graduates available to fill them.

K-12 students are a critical piece of this solution. Organizations like Black Girls Code and movies like Black Panther have been so important in showing Black women and girls of all ages that they belong in a field where (for far too long) they've only seen White and Asian men. It does my heart good to hear so many young ladies proudly say they want to be like Shuri! We're being inspired to become the creators (not just the consumers) of technology.

With all of this amazing work being done, there's still a critical need. As you learn more about computing, take more classes, choose a major, and eventually enter your career, there are the "other" important lessons that aren't taught in a course. How do you handle the rejection, failure, implicit bias, and more that you'll encounter? How do we, as Black women in computing, ensure that you, the next generation, are properly armored to persist in the field and be the unapologetically dope women you're destined to be?

It's my hope that *this* book becomes your roadmap. You won't learn a thing about programming, networking, security, or anything else computing related after reading this. In fact, you don't need to be a computer science major (or Black) to get something from this book. This advice is probably just as relevant and apropos if you're a woman of any race or ethnicity in any other field. However, as a Black woman in computing, this is my truth. That's all I can speak from. What you *will* learn from this book are the things that help you not only reach your goals, but also exceed them. It's designed for that moment when you're automatically labeled as intimidating, angry, or aggressive because you're assertive and confident of your skills. It's also for that moment when you're doubted by a teacher, professor, peer, or supervisor who thinks you don't belong, simply because you're a Black woman. Finally, it's for that moment when you realize you're no longer in Kansas, and it's truly "sink or swim." In those moments, when you aren't sure what to think, say, or do, I hope this book becomes your resource to helping you become and remember the unapologetically dope woman you are.

What better person to help you navigate this journey than someone who's also lived it? My story was more of an exception than the rule though. My mother (a math major) spent 37 years at IBM as a computer programmer and manager, so I didn't have to look far for role models. I grew up with a computer in my house from as young as I can remember, and I was programming before high school. I majored in computer science (CS) at Johnson C. Smith University [a Historically Black College and University (HBCU) in Charlotte, NC], and I completed my master's and doctoral degrees from North Carolina State University. I spent nine years at IBM as a software engineering intern, from my senior year of high school to my last year of my Ph.D. I've worked in both industry and academia, including The Aerospace Corporation, nine years in the Department of Computer Science at Howard University, and most recently, Winthrop University. From the first time I stepped foot on Johnson C. Smith's campus to now, the one consistency is that I've done things my way. I never conformed to the mold of being "typical," and it's been my life's work to change the narrative of what (more importantly, *who*) a computer scientist looks like. Here's where you come into the story.

I'm so blessed to have reached a point in my career where I not only have knowledge and wisdom to share, but also (more importantly) that I can share it with the growing number of you I see entering the field and doing amazing things. There's a wealth of lessons I've learned over the past 20 years, none of which are directly related to computing. However, they've all helped me face challenges and progress both academically and professionally. Some things I learned from my mother, mentors, and professors who "got it." They knew how to handle many challenges because they'd personally faced them. Other things I had to learn the hard way.

I chose to share some of the most hilarious, confusing, enraging, and heartbreaking moments of my life in these pages, with the hope that it helps someone else who may experience the same. Life happens, and it's full of twists and turns that we never expected. At 40 years old, even I have to laugh at how completely wrong and limited my plans were for myself at ages 20 and 30.

What I can tell you is that, through it all, it's been an amazing journey! I couldn't have made it to where I am without the love and support of so many people. There's no way I could name them all, but I DO want to mention a few before I go any further. First and foremost, I have to thank my mother for showing me the power of Black girl magic decades before it was even a thing, and for always being an amazing sounding board for any career advice

I've needed over the years. A special shout out goes to Brenda Darden Wilkerson and Pat Yongpradit, for the amazing work you have done and continue to do. Thank you for being so supportive of this journey. Last but not least, I have to give a major thanks to my friend Nikia Harrod-Long, for reminding me daily to focus on what mattered (like finishing this book)! All I can say is WHEW!!! Muva made it!

To each and every one of you reading this book, I hope you gain some free jewelry that helps you sit up just a little straighter, speak just a little more confidently, and walk just a little taller and with a little more swagger. May you have the audacity to be unapologetic, dope, and most importantly, yourself.

Have a Plan

First things first, you need a plan. What's your end game? What are your goals? What do you want to accomplish in life: educationally, professionally, and personally? I include personally in this list because, too often, we develop a detailed plan for our educational and professional pursuits. Yet, when it comes to our personal lives, we never give it the serious thought it deserves.

This isn't to say that your plans will all come to fruition. Life happens, of course, and as the saying goes, "If you want to make God laugh, tell him your plans." We can plan every day of our lives for the next 20 years, and everything can go completely left in the blink of an eye. Still, it's good to have some idea of what you want to accomplish. The most successful people don't just happen upon their success. They set goals and worked to achieve them. Sometimes they faced an unexpected detour and adversity. However, they adjusted their course and pushed forward.

Before you dive any further into this book, think about what you want to accomplish. Why are you pursuing a degree or career in computing? This deserves some serious thought. One of the things I often ask students is, "Why did you choose CS as a major?" The range of answers typically includes:

- "I always loved computers." (Translation: I love to *use* computers.)
- "I'm good at computers." (Translation: I'm pretty good at using social media and computer applications.)

7

- I can make a lot of money."
- "My family told me I should major in it."
- "I've never taken any courses, but I'm curious to learn more about it."
- "I took CS courses in high school and really liked it."

Very rarely do I hear the last two answers. More often than not, it's the first four. This usually isn't a good sign, if I'm being completely honest. If I tallied every student who responded with one of those answers, then I'm almost certain 95% of them found that the major wasn't what they thought it would be and chose to pursue something else.

The issue with their disillusionment is not always that they didn't properly identify a plan. They could've still been successful, had they received the appropriate support and resources to help them learn more about the field. It's not their fault though. Too many colleges and universities require incoming freshmen to declare a major when applying. How many of us *actually* knew what we wanted to major in as a high-school senior? Only recently have K-12 CS initiatives become a national focus. Prior to this, very few schools had CS courses that adequately prepared students for undergraduate programs. I was certain until my second semester of my freshman year of college that I wanted to major in marketing. By my senior year, I had *no* clue what I wanted to do career-wise. I only knew what I *didn't* want to do, which was sit in front of a computer programming all day.

Having said that, it's a good idea to start thinking about your immediate, short-term, and long-term goals. What do you want to accomplish over the next year, 3-5 years, and 7-10 years? Create a journal, vision board, or file, and list your goals by category (education, career, personal). Of course, these will probably change. Nothing is set in stone, so feel free to be as inspired as you want. The key is that these are no longer just random thoughts in your head. You've made them tangible and something to work towards.

Once you identify these goals, then determine your plan of action. Start with the immediate goals over the next year. What will you do to ensure that you move one step closer each day, week, and month to achieving them? Is it taking a course, researching a topic, or saving money? How will you measure your progress?

Your short-term goals provide you a little more flexibility, as they will most likely occur in the next 3-5 years. Is it completing a degree, obtaining a promotion, or planning for a family? Remember, there is no rule requiring your personal goals to be placed on hold in order to achieve your educational and professional ones. Whatever they are, list them (somewhere), and have an idea of how to progress towards reaching them. Finally, the same should apply to your long-term goals. Depending on where you are in your academic and/or professional career, this could mean beginning your career or moving into more senior-level positions.

The key to truly being successful is to *plan* to be. Luck is when preparation meets opportunity. The most successful people create their own luck. My senior year of college was filled with partying, classes, and determining what I wanted to do (or not do) when I graduated. I had a job offer from IBM, but I'd determined (with my mother's advice) that I should attend graduate school and pursue a master's degree.

While home for fall break, I received a phone call from Dr. Dorothy Yancy, the university president. She informed me that she was nominating me for the David and Lucille Packard Fellowship, a five-year, $100,000 award to HBCU graduates pursuing Ph.D.'s in science, technology, engineering, and math (STEM). I remember my response to her was, "Thanks Dr. Yancy, but I don't want to do a Ph.D. I'm only planning on doing a master's." In no uncertain terms did she tell me, "Nicki, I'm nominating you anyway. The worst-case scenario is that you get the award and decide not to accept it. Send me your resume. This is too important."

I'd learned over the prior 3.5 years that when Dr. Yancy tells you she's doing something, you just fall in line. I emailed my resume to her that evening and completed my application before I returned to campus. Suffice it to say that I was chosen as a 2000 Packard Fellow, and the rest was history. My point: When you stay ready, you don't have to get ready. What many people may see as someone's "luck" is really the culmination of years of hard work, perseverance, and preparation manifesting itself at the opportune time.

I challenge you to take a moment and think about at least one goal for each of these timelines (immediate, short-term, and long-term). It will help you as you complete the rest of this book, as you'll be able to leverage the people, resources, and opportunities you encounter to help you along your journey. Remember, failing to plan is planning to fail. So what are you waiting on?

Assemble Your Tribe

Before you get knee deep into this book, I have to emphasize how absolutely essential this life lesson is on so many levels. A major part of being a successful Black woman in the tech field includes surrounding yourself with a group of people who unapologetically support you, hold you accountable, and help you become the best version of yourself possible.

The poet John Donne wrote, "No man is an island entire of itself." This is even truer for us as Black women, especially in computing. None of us are here solely by our own merits. We stand not only on the backs of those who came before us, but also in front of those who are behind the scenes holding us up when we can't gather ourselves, pushing us forward when we are too scared to take the first step, and believing in us when we have lost all confidence.

Your tribe is everything. Let me say that a little louder for the folks in the back. Your. Tribe. Is. *EVERYTHING*. T-Mobile had a commercial that asked, "Who's in your five?" Who are the five people you communicate with the most? These people are your tribe. They have the most influence on you personally and professionally, so choose wisely. While you will inevitably (or hopefully) have a circle that consists of more than five people, it's imperative that these five *types* of people are a part of your team.

The Sage

This person is the one who has the experience to help you navigate any path you find yourself on. She's traveled your journey and understands firsthand what you've been through, what you're currently facing, and what's just around the corner, because she *is* you. The Sage is typically in your field (or one with similar challenges). She may be older, the same age, or in some cases, younger. For this woman, age is truly nothing but a number because she's wise beyond her years.

The Sage will often serve as your voice of reason. She's learned to play the game and she's thriving. She'll offer constructive criticism on what you could be doing better to address any challenges and also serve as a sounding board to vent your frustrations and concerns. Trust her insight. Her advice is designed to help you learn from her lessons, both good and bad. Unfortunately, you may still face similar ones (we *are* still Black women in the tech field, mind you). However, she will help you take comfort in the fact that you weren't the first and surely won't be the last.

The Straight Shooter

This chick. Brace yourself. She's the one who is 100% unfiltered and unapologetic about it. Everything she tells you is from a place of love; never doubt that. However, the delivery can be a bit…interesting…and off-putting at times. You are guaranteed to hate this woman at *least* three times per year, because you're going to make the mistake of calling her when you feel completely defeated and she's going to upset you even more within 10 minutes of conversation. Heed my warning, she is NOT. HERE. FOR. YOUR. PITY. PARTY. Not today, not tomorrow, not ever.

The beauty of having The Straight Shooter on your team is that, despite what you think, you actually *need* her brashness. It's important to remember that she *always* has your back. She just won't hold your hand and let you play the victim. She may let you cry, whine, or complain for approximately five minutes, but her next response will be, "OK, that's about enough of that. What's the game plan?" The Straight Shooter keeps you grounded. She's that outer gut check that helps you put everything back into perspective at just the right time. She reminds you that there's a greater purpose, that you're doper than you realize (at that moment), and helps you toughen yourself up to get ready for the next battle you face. God bless her.

The Cheerleader

This person is truly your biggest fan. Remember how bad you felt the moment you realized you shouldn't have called The Straight Shooter to complain about that problem? The Cheerleader is the person you probably wish you'd called instead. She will always have an uplifting and inspirational word for anything you discuss, good or bad. She has a comforting spirit that makes you feel at ease, even when your anxiety is through the roof.

One of the best qualities of this woman is that she will always remind you of just how amazing you are. If you want to cry, go ahead, she has an ear. If someone frustrated you and you just want to vent, she'll listen to that as well. She will never let you doubt or be too hard on yourself. She won't offer advice unless it's solicited, because she's more concerned that you're OK with you. When things are great, The Cheerleader is high-fiving you every step of the way. However, when things aren't so great, she reminds you of all the wonderful ways in which you're an amazing woman and will never let you forget it.

The Motivator

This is the person who provides you healthy and friendly competition. She's often a person in your field or a different one with similar goals. You two are probably very close in age, because you're both pursuing the same things educationally, professionally, and maybe personally. The Motivator is driven, focused, and hungry. She inspires and pushes you to persevere, not because of anything that she specifically says, but just by virtue of being herself. You witness her grind and instantly follow suit.

One of the best qualities of The Motivator is that she probably views you from the same perspective. The two of you may even eventually collaborate. You both respect each other's hustle, and as interdisciplinary as the tech field is, you'll easily find ways in which the two of you can work together to build something phenomenal. This is the woman who reminds you that you're gradually assembling a team that can eventually take over the world. Keep grinding.

The Plug

The Plug is the connector. She knows anyone and everyone. If you even mention an idea to The Plug, then she knows *just* the person to help you get started. Her next words are usually, "How can I help?" She's an amazing and trusted resource, because she has a wealth of knowledge about how to get started, who to talk to, and what your next steps should be. She'll even connect you to the right people or someone who can get you to them.

One of the best qualities of The Plug is that she loves to help people. It's one of the reasons that she *is* so well connected. She's done amazing things in her career and wants to ensure that others have the same opportunities to thrive. In some cases, she may also be The Sage. When you meet this woman and she offers assistance, then TAKE ADVANTAGE OF IT. She's more than ready and willing to help. Remember, closed mouths don't get fed.

There's one thing I hope you paid attention to in reading about each of these tribe members: They are all women (and preferably Black). While your tribe may consist of more people of different genders, ethnicities, and races, it's important that at *least* five of these individuals are Black women who fit each of the aforementioned descriptions. Remember, they don't all have to be in computing. They just need to be Black women who can provide you the nourishment needed to not just survive, but also thrive.

As you grow both professionally and personally, you'll meet more people from more diverse backgrounds, and your tribe will shift and expand in ways you didn't expect and couldn't imagine. I'm eternally grateful for my tribe of Black women who have helped me become the woman I am today and will be tomorrow. They've wiped many a tear, served many a read, and given many a praise dance for me. To each of you (you know who you are), I want to say thank you from the absolute bottom of my heart. We are all continuous works in progress. However, this thing called life is so much easier and more beautiful when you know you have genuine people surrounding you with nothing but unconditional love.

Twice as Good is Still the Rule

God bless Shonda Rhimes. Any Black person of a certain age who watched *Scandal* knows how apropos Eli Pope's monologues to Olivia were, because we often heard the same from our parents growing up. One of the most memorable was the family motto he promptly reminded Olivia of: "You have to be twice as good as them to get half of what they have."

Translation: As a Black person in this country, you *cannot* afford to do "just enough" to get by. The rules aren't the same for us as they are for others. Unfortunately, we're reminded of that daily in every aspect of our lives, from being stopped by the police to simply trying to swim in our neighborhood pools. If these issues are happening at home, do you think they aren't happening in school or at work as well?

My parents were raised in the Jim Crow south. They understood all too well that it didn't matter how smart or accomplished you were. To some people, you would always be viewed as beneath them. They reminded me every day that it never mattered what the minimum academic requirements of my school or teams were, as their requirements were always much higher. A grade of a C was never allowed on my report card. If I earned a B in a class, then that was only because I poured everything I had into it and that was the best I could do. Otherwise, if I could've earned an A and didn't, then there would be problems.

This type of standard wasn't because my mother was a Tiger Mom. It was because she built her entire career in corporate

America from the early 1970s to early 2000s. She'd experienced racism since she was a child and understood that as much as she excelled, she'd still risk losing out to a White man or woman with less accomplishments, experience, and credentials than her. She taught me that the same rules for everyone else never applied to me. More was *always* expected. Whatever the baseline was, mine was *always* set much higher.

I'm amazed at the number of young Black students I speak to now who were never taught this mantra. Part of what I loved about teaching at Howard was that I could have these "come-to-Jesus" moments with my entire class on any given day. They may not have wanted to hear it, but eventually, most of them came to understand it. One summer, a certain well-known tech company hired one of our undergraduates for an internship. He nailed it, completing multiple projects during the summer when most interns only completed one. This company didn't hire him for full-time employment, because we later learned that they didn't think he was a "good fit." I should note, this student was (at the time) a quiet and reserved young man and was always respectful and friendly. I can assure you that the average engineer does *not* have anywhere near a gregarious personality.

A few years later, a manager from the same company all but offered me a position that she acknowledged I was "exceptionally qualified" for in our phone interview. In fact, she fast-tracked the onsite interview to four days later, as it was just "a formality." All of a sudden, two days after human resources contacted me to schedule my travel arrangements, I received an email stating, "The position is no longer available." There was no explanation, no apologies, nothing. I immediately emailed that same manager, who never responded. It was only after someone else I knew who worked there inquired about it that I learned that I too wasn't considered a good fit. Someone noted this in an interview two years prior. While negative reviews from a prior interview could disqualify a candidate, the current hiring manager could have overridden this and still onboarded me if she wanted to. However, she didn't want to ruffle any feathers. Even more egregious was the fact that she didn't have the decency to respond to my email regarding it.

In both of these examples, we all know what a "good fit" really meant. While the phrasing may change, the meaning never does. During Reconstruction and Jim Crow, some of our ancestors were called "uppity" because they didn't know how to "stay in their place." Sound familiar? There's enough articles about the lack of diversity in Silicon Valley at this point that make it very clear that not fitting in a company culture is code speak for "too Black" or more so "not what we normally see or want around here." I still question the intentions of companies that claim to be serious about diversity, yet do nothing to eradicate practices that are designed to deny Black applicants. How are the same people who took no issue with keeping applicants out going to not only understand what it takes to properly recruit Black talent, but also (more importantly) *want* to now recruit them? The same people who didn't want us now know what it takes to get more of us in the door? I digress though.

Even as an experienced professional in my career, I still follow the "twice-as-good" rule. As a Black woman in higher education, I am often critiqued *first* by some students based on my perceived "attitude." Specifically, because I'm direct and hold students accountable, that makes me rude. However, the same tone and expectations from a colleague of another gender or race/ethnicity are perceived as "tough, but fair."

If class starts at 11 a.m., then my doors are locked at 11 a.m. and late entries are prohibited. I explain during the first week of class that this is for numerous reasons. First, because of active shooter risks, the doors are locked to provide an extra barrier of protection for everyone inside the classroom, should an event occur. In the current world we live in, this shouldn't even require explanation. Second, if the class starts at 11 a.m., then students should be there and ready at 11 a.m. They can't show up five minutes late to a job interview and tell a potential employer that they couldn't find parking, there was traffic, or they overslept. They've lost before they even had a chance. Finally, I can't show up to class five minutes late every day and blame traffic, parking, or anything else. Otherwise, students will complain to their parents, my department chair, the dean, or higher. As such, we will all honor the commitment we've made to be in class and on time.

This sounds like a pretty rational explanation, right? However, at the end of every semester, some students complain on evaluations that I'm rude, I lock the door and don't allow them to arrive even a few minutes late, and I don't accept late assignments. The irony in all of these complaints is that they don't focus on the content or instruction. No one complaining acknowledges that I record lectures and post the audio to help them review after class. They don't discuss how I encourage each of them to pursue internships and other opportunities, even offering to review resumes outside of class. No one complaining mentions that I spend time in office hours and via email helping students review problems or make every topic as relevant as possible to ensure everyone understands the concepts. They don't remind themselves (or anyone they complain to) that this is exactly what will be expected of them in the real world, and I've repeatedly reminded them of this. Of course, those who complain also never discuss how they may call any man in the building "Dr. Whoever," yet I'm often referred to as "Ms." or "Mrs. Washington." When I correct them on this (after noting this in the first week of class as well), then of course I'm rude (again). Instead, they focus on things that really shouldn't matter, because I should be nicer and more approachable.

Pause.

In essence, I shouldn't have the audacity to be me and expect others to respect me. I could cite the plethora of literature discussing Black women in higher education and the negative perceptions that are automatically associated with them, especially on student evaluations. I could talk about the conversations I've had with colleagues who acknowledge there's nothing that different in how we engage with the students, other than our gender and/or race. I won't waste time with that. My point in discussing this is that if I did just the bare minimum to get through class (office hours, grading, and teaching), then I would be considered an even more terrible professor by some students. I literally go above and beyond expectations to *still* have to defend myself as a professor.

Is this absurd? Absolutely. Is it a hill worth dying on? ABSOLUTELY. It's a battle I will continue to fight because someone reading this will be interested in pursuing a career in academia. Others will be interested in pursuing a career in industry. With either route, you may face the exact same misperceptions of you. You will be questioned (directly or indirectly) as to why you are there. People will expect less of you; yet simultaneously hold you to a higher standard than even they can reach. Persist anyway. If the requirement is two projects to complete, then submit four. If everyone else is doing the bare minimum, then go above and beyond. Most importantly, ensure that no one can ever *truly* question your abilities, because they will anyway. However, facts and results are hard to debate or dispute.

Play Chess When Everyone Else is Playing Checkers

I can always find a song lyric that is apropos for any situation or mood. One of my favorites is from the hip hop artist T.I., which states, "Life is like a chess move. You need to make your next move your best move." Every decision you make should always bring you closer to your end goal.

Strategy is such an important part of your success. As Black women, we are still such a minority in computing that we must remember to play the game at times to get what we want and/or need. It's great to be unapologetically you. However, finesse and strategy are important for successfully navigating this field.

Identify the Power Players and Gatekeepers

I was fortunate enough to be an INROADS alumnus (NC-RTP) from 1996-2000. With the goal of addressing the lack of diversity in corporate America, INROADS participants not only were paid interns at major companies across the country, but also received professional development opportunities that would help us throughout our academic and professional careers.

I remember one workshop that discussed the importance of identifying the power players and gatekeepers of any organization. The power players are those individuals who are responsible for the direction of the organization. They have significant influence because of their position and accomplishments, and they are usually well respected and trusted by everyone. These include the CEOs, managers, department chairs, deans, presidents, and other senior administrators. They also can include other non-administrative colleagues who've garnered a reputation for their internal and external contributions to the organization. These are the individuals whose radars you want to be on. They should know you and your work before they've met you, as they have the ability to help you get to the next level.

Equally as important as the power players are the gatekeepers. These aren't the people responsible for the direction and operation of the organization. Instead, they're the staff (such as administrative assistants, network administrators, maintenance, and custodians) that provides access to those people, resources, and opportunities. If you pay close enough attention, you'll quickly realize that these individuals are the ones responsible for the organization's successful daily operations.

For this reason, it's important to ensure that you maintain a respectful and courteous relationship with the gatekeepers, just as you would the power players. Over the past 20 years, I've witnessed one too many a credentialed colleague cozy up to the power players, yet look down upon and speak in a condescending tone to gatekeepers. Always remember, it costs you nothing to be a decent person and treat people with respect. Besides, you attract more flies with honey than vinegar.

Avoid the Toxic Colleagues

We've all encountered at least one person we work with who is unbearable. He/she complains about everything, finds the negative in every situation, and constantly has an issue with at least two other people. These people are often the same ones who are constantly the victim, always looking to get over, and/or bullying someone else. Steer clear of these people. No matter how accomplished they are, their reputations will always precede them. You never want to be associated with their drama, so maintain a cordial-yet-distant professional relationship.

Play the Game

Some of the biggest areas where we, as Black women, often miss out on opportunities are the "unofficial" work events. These are the times that are considered "off the clock," but they are really informal gatherings where critical connections or deals are made. These include the after-work happy hour, round of golf, weekend celebration at a colleague's house, or even lunch. Sometimes it's because we aren't invited. Other times, it's because we choose not to attend. In either case, you must learn to include yourself.

My last year of graduate school, my mother bought me a set of golf lessons as a Christmas gift. She told me that one of her biggest regrets in her career at IBM was that she never learned how to play golf. She knew that she was being left out of certain informal meetings and opportunities as a result of this, and she never wanted me to miss any opportunities because I didn't know how to play. Even if I didn't play well, the point was to be comfortable enough to *be present* with anyone else.

That gift, conversation, and lesson stuck with me to this day, and I often remind other Black women of it when discussing the importance of stepping outside of their comfort zones and "playing the game." It's one thing to not be invited. However, you do yourself a disservice when you *are* invited, yet choose to not participate. Don't get me wrong; life happens, and if you're a parent or have other obligations, then you can't always make these events. However, if you have the opportunity, then you should *always* take it. It may mean paying for a sitter sometimes, not being able to go home and decompress right after work, or being around people you don't think you have much in common with. Remember, the end justifies the means. These events not only provide you access to certain conversations, opportunities, and people, but also allow others to see you as collegial and a team player.

So what do you do in the event that you're *not* invited? How do you gain access to these opportunities? That answer is simple: You invite yourself. That's right. You make yourself welcome to some of the easily accessible events, and eventually work your way into the other ones. For example, who's stopping you from grabbing lunch with colleagues? On my campus, a subset of faculty always eats in the cafeteria for lunch. When I first arrived, I knew no one there, and would quickly grab my lunch to go, so that I could prep for my next class, especially on the days where I had exactly one hour to eat between classes. However, on the days when my schedule was more flexible, I'd either stop by colleagues' offices to ask if they were going to lunch or ask to join them when I found them in the cafeteria. I now regularly eat with this same group and welcome new colleagues to join us as well.

Sometimes it's really as simple as taking the initiative. These are small entry points into larger circles. Casual conversations often happen over a meal. People discuss travel, hobbies, weekend plans, and more. These all become opportunities to then invite yourself OR actually be invited to other events. Someone mentions they're playing a round of golf? Simply mention, "I play golf as well. I've been looking to get out there more. Mind if I join you one day?" You'd be amazed at how most people won't tell you no, even if they want to. If a group mentions hanging out at a restaurant or bar after work, then ask to join them.

Disclaimer: If attending a happy hour or event where alcohol is served, avoid drinking. I've seen one too many work-related events that included alcohol, and let's just say that some people forgot they were actually with their coworkers. Don't be those people.

My point is that there are a number of non-work-related activities where work is still discussed or occurring. So many times in the past, we've been left out of these opportunities or chose to avoid them altogether. We can't afford to continue to make these kinds of decisions. Remember to always play chess.

Here's another example that bridges the idea of identifying the power players and playing the game. I was fortunate enough as a graduate student to receive several fellowships. At the time, most of the recipients were Black and Latino students, all pursuing their master's or doctoral degrees in STEM.

One summer during our annual symposium, another participant mentioned the challenges he was facing as a Ph.D. student. His original advisor left the university, and his new one had some professional and personal issues with another member of his dissertation committee. As a result, his research and defense were stalled because of the differences between his committee members. It reached a point where he was so frustrated that he eventually transferred to his original advisor's new university. However, his time to completion was further delayed, as he couldn't transfer all of his credits.

This was a nightmare situation that I remember vividly as a third-year graduate student. There was *no* way that I would allow myself to end up in a similar situation. When the time came to select my dissertation committee (three additional faculty), I remember my advisor asking who I wanted to solicit. I strategically identified every member of my committee based on two things: 1) their interactions with my advisor, and 2) their interactions with me. The first was a junior faculty member in the department who was in a similar research area as my advisor. Because he was junior faculty, being a member of a dissertation committee helped his tenure portfolio. He also had a great relationship with my advisor. The second member was a professor who was somewhat of a mentee to my advisor. The third member was a professor whose research was the foundation of mine and also taught two of my favorite graduate courses. He was also a very good friend of my advisor's. This is what I mean about strategizing. I wanted zero problems during my research or defense, and the only way to ensure that was to ensure that every member of my committee liked and respected each other as well as me.

I should note, there was one professor my advisor suggested for my committee that was a hard no for me. I'd met him when searching for an advisor at the end of my first year of graduate school. You will learn more about him later in this book. In short, he didn't think that I could "cut it" as his graduate researcher. In no uncertain terms, I told my advisor that I would absolutely *not* ask him for anything, and then told him about our initial encounter. My advisor immediately agreed this was not a good choice, apologized for that person's rudeness, and told me I made a wise decision by not interacting with him anymore.

Say Little and Do the Most

One of my favorite quotes is from *American Gangster*, when Denzel Washington's character (Frank Lucas) tells his brother, "The loudest one in the room is the weakest one in the room." His brother was overly extravagant and ostentatious at the time, buying flashy clothes and jewelry and being "extra." The same mantra should be applied regularly in everything you do. If you have to talk about what you're doing all the time, then you're *probably* not doing that much. Stay humble and hungry. No one needs to know your every move. Let your work speak for itself. Keep quiet, be aware of your environment (and how it operates), play the game, and keep grinding. Believe me, your work will precede you in the best ways possible.

Know Your Allies from Your Adversaries

Remember how we previously discussed being strategic, specifically, playing chess when others are playing checkers? Consider this nugget of wisdom supplementary information. It's important to understand who your allies versus adversaries are. Regardless of whether you're enrolled in school or working, you need to identify individuals who are internal to the organization and have a vested interest in helping you succeed. You also need to be aware of those who may (directly or indirectly) impede your growth.

You can easily identify your allies if you pay close enough attention. They may be faculty, department chairs, mentors, administrators, or staff (if you're a student), or coworkers, mentors, or supervisors (if you're a professional). You're usually a little more comfortable confiding in them, because they've previously demonstrated that they are trustworthy and have your best interests at heart.

Alternately, your adversaries are those who may exhibit a clear oppositional approach to you (directly or indirectly), don't appear the most trustworthy, or are extremely confrontational. I should note that identification of both adversaries and allies requires careful, objective observations on your part. You may also get a sense of a person's character from casual conversations that you hear about them. Notice I said, "that you hear." Don't play the gossip game with people. Quietly listen and cautiously observe. You can usually make an informed decision based on what you witness.

For example, if most students who recently or never met me were to take the advice of a certain group of students who've completed my courses, then they would think I was rude, mean, condescending, and unwilling to bend. However, if they speak to the other group of students about me (or more importantly, sat down to have a conversation with me during office hours), then they'd realize that I have high expectations of students because I give them the highest possible effort I have. I always preface my expectations with, "You play how you practice," and I continuously remind them that I'm grooming them for interviews, internships, and full-time employment opportunities. They'd even learn that I love to joke and interact with students.

I once had several young women come to me in confidence that a colleague made a derogatory comment about the programming abilities of female students. Specifically, he didn't think they were as capable as male students. It was clear that each of these young women, who I'd previously taught, felt comfortable enough discussing their concerns with me. That in itself is enough to make me feel like I did something right. However, after asking each of them how they wanted to handle it, they were unsure. None of them felt comfortable confronting the professor, because naturally, they didn't want their grade to be affected. I assured them that would never happen, and to be sure it didn't, they needed to appropriately and immediately document the event, as I would also be doing. I then asked was each of them okay with me addressing it. They all agreed.

At the next department meeting, I mentioned the current climate, specifically how some faculty were discouraging female students with disparaging comments. I then discussed how several young women came to me with their concerns, but were uncomfortable addressing the professor directly because they did not want it to affect their grades. As one of only two women (and the only Black woman) in the department, it was imperative that I spoke up for these young women, as I had the ability to not only hold colleagues accountable, but also make it known to the men in the department that these types of statements would absolutely not be tolerated.

As a Black woman, it would've been very remiss of me to *not* speak up for those students. I'm forever grateful that they were comfortable enough to come to me with their concerns, and they also trusted me to appropriately address them in a manner that ensured they never had to endure such foolishness again from anyone else or risk being impacted for standing up for themselves (at least within the department).

To this day, I always quietly listen and cautiously observe the actions of those around me to identify who fits into which bucket (ally or adversary). We all need to know we aren't alone. Despite how marginalized or isolated you feel, know that there is someone you can identify as an ally. If you're having trouble determining who that is, then I suggest you speak to your tribe member, The Sage. She can usually help you discern who you should look to for the internal support you will surely need to navigate any organization.

Closed Mouths Don't Get Fed

Have you ever heard the saying, "The squeaky wheel gets the oil?" Think of any vehicle in operation. If maintenance is needed, the wheel that makes the most noise is the one that gets fixed first. Have you ever wondered why that person who's a little more vocal than everyone else always seems to be the one who gets everything that he/she requests?

It's because that's the person that people remember, the person making the "fuss." That's also the person who usually gets his/her needs met well before anyone else. This is why I tell students (and professionals) to speak up and out. Sit in the front of the class or conference room. Ask and answer questions. Make yourself known, for the *right* reasons.

As a student, your teachers and professors should know you by name before the midpoint of the semester. This means you're unafraid to speak up in class, come to office hours, and/or ask questions. *You* are the first student who's remembered when an email is received that requests nominations for a scholarship or internship. You always want to be *that* student.

As a professional, your colleagues should know you by name for the same reasons. You're the one who not only gets things done, but also makes things happen. You don't sit around and wait for others to do it. You speak up when necessary and are unafraid and unapologetic to make your voice known. This is mainly because you know what you're doing and that it's all for the right reasons. Ultimately, everyone around you has to admit that as well.

I once found myself getting stalled at work because other people in the pipeline hadn't approved or processed something. I needed approvals for summer salaries, student tuition or stipends, or travel authorizations and reimbursements. Given that none of these could afford to wait that long, I often had to pick up a phone and call people, walk to their office, or worse, involve a superior, in order to get the ball rolling. This happened more times than I can count. Every time it happened, I was just as vocal as the last. I understood that there were people's livelihoods on the line. Those processed payments meant a student could pay their rent or eat, and timely processing of financial aid meant that their classes didn't get purged. As a single woman with a one-income household, my savings and emergency funds were my only resource, should I not get paid on time. I never wanted to be in that situation, so I made sure I never put others in it.

For that reason, I always made sure that I spoke up and out for anyone I was responsible for. I needed to ensure that they had what they needed so that they could complete the work I needed. You *must* be unafraid to speak up and out for yourself (and sometimes others). At the end of the day, no one will fight for you like you will. Don't sell yourself short when you know you deserve more or better.

Know Your Worth

We are often taught, "Know your worth, then add tax," when it comes to our personal lives, but why are we not taught the same for our professional lives? Why aren't we taught as adamantly to never settle when it comes to our careers? Just as in our personal relationships, we have to understand what we bring to the table professionally and not allow others to devalue that. Do you actually know what you're worth? Are you confident and audacious enough to ask for it when you're hired for a new job or not getting it in your current one? Are you willing to walk away when you feel undervalued and unappreciated?

This is often an uncomfortable topic to discuss for many of us, regardless of our field. However, this is one of the areas where we must develop the confidence and audacity to ask for our worth and expect it. Black women earn 63 cents to every dollar that White men earn. That's a *huge* discrepancy. This translates to a Black woman having to work a little over 1.5 years in order to earn the same amount that a White man earned in one year. How do we change this?

First, we start by truly understanding what we bring to the table. Your resume speaks for itself. Sadly, as a woman (a Black woman), the same resume with a man's name will probably garner him higher compensation. You must know and be willing to articulate (to yourself and anyone else) what you bring to the table. Second, understand what someone with your qualifications should be earning. Thankfully, there are a ton of websites that discuss the average salaries of various positions based on location and seniority. There are also websites that present this information by company. If you work for a federal or state-funded organization, then you can find current salaries of all employees via federal or state databases. This will often help you determine what someone in that position currently earns, to understand what you *should* be earning.

Next, don't be afraid to *ask* for what you're worth. Always remember to negotiate when you're offered a new job or position. My mother taught me to never accept the first offer. Something is always negotiable, even when you think it isn't. I've talked to many women who admitted that they never negotiated their salaries because they feared that simply asking for more or to start the discussion would result in a rescinded offer. This can be a costly assumption. Once you've received an offer, it is perfectly acceptable to ask, "Is this negotiable?" The worst that you will be told is no. However, what you often hear is something to the extent of, "I'm unsure. There isn't much room for adjustments. What were you looking for?" This is why it's important to do your homework. Ask for time to make an acceptable counteroffer, then present your request. If rationale is needed, then be prepared to present that as well. If you're requesting a raise or promotion as a current employee, then you should definitely be prepared to provide the justification for your request. "No" is the worst you will hear.

Finally, if you're asked or expected to work for less than what you deserve, then don't be afraid to decline an offer. All money ain't good money. As a consultant, I've often been asked to lower my fees to "work with" someone's budget. I have no problem declining these opportunities at this point in my career. I've worked way too hard and have amassed a resume that is way too lengthy to be expected to compromise my worth. If someone wants to hire me, then they will pay what I expect. Otherwise, they won't work with me. It's as simple as that. I also won't go above and beyond to explain to someone why I'm worth my fee. If my resume isn't enough to convince you, then nothing is. In that case, I'm good.

Think about when you've settled for less than you knew you deserved in a personal relationship. Most of us, if we're honest, will acknowledge that we've done this at least once in our lives. How did you feel, knowing that you deserved more? Did you feel satisfied or appreciated? Were you completely happy with yourself, or were you disappointed? Remember that feeling when someone asks you to do the same professionally. Will you be appreciated? Will you be completely happy with yourself, knowing that you're expected to still perform high-quality work for lower pay? Probably not. You will know that you sold yourself short, and once you allow yourself to be devalued, it's hard to ever convince that same person that you are worth much more. Don't waste your time or money. Better yet, don't let *others* waste it.

Hold People (Including Yourself) Accountable

Part of knowing your worth means that you must hold everyone, including yourself, accountable. You should be warned that not everyone will like or appreciate this accountability. That's not your problem. It's your responsibility, as your (and sometimes others') greatest advocate, to make the hard and unpopular decision.

For some reason, my sixth-grade math teacher (a White woman) decided to have a class discussion on the relevance of Black History Month. I still cram to understand why people decide to take this upon themselves and then get upset when the responses aren't what they expected. I can't remember the exact discussion, but it centered on me arguing why Black History Month was needed and why White History Month didn't need to be a thing. What I *do* remember from this discussion was my teacher looking at me with pity and saying in a condescending tone, "Oh Alicia, it's people like you that give Blacks a bad rep."

Pause.

I was 12 years old. This was an adult telling a 12-year-old child something so egregious, not because she was wrong, but because she dared to disagree with her. I remember the anger and embarrassment I felt at being told this by my teacher, and I chose to remain quiet for the rest of the day…until I got home. Once I was in the car with my mom, I relayed the story to her in detail. The look of shock, confusion, and anger was apparent on her face. She asked me at least three times if I was positive that my version of the conversation was accurate. As most of you know, when it comes to Black parents, if they have to show up at the school, then you better make *sure* they know the entire story and you did nothing wrong. Otherwise, there will be an entire world of problems awaiting you at home. After I promised repeatedly that this story was accurate, I also informed my mother of other random conversations this woman thought appropriate to share with her sixth-grade math class, including how she and her husband were having problems getting pregnant.

Pause…again.

If you're wondering why any sixth-grade teacher thought this appropriate to discuss with her class, then trust me, you aren't and weren't alone. I couldn't fully understand the level of inappropriateness of it all. However, thank goodness Reggie and De Washington did. After my dad (a K-12 administrator) calmed my mom down, they both devised a strategy on how to tackle this, and my mother promptly requested a meeting with the principal and teacher.

Even the principal (a Black man) was so taken aback by the allegations that he called me into the conference with my mom and teacher to explain exactly what happened. I retold the "bad rep" story, as well as the numerous times this teacher mentioned how hard she and her husband were trying to have a baby. Suffice it to say that, not long after I arrived, this woman was in complete tears (no surprise there). My mother's borderline-calm rage and the principal's shock and disgust resulted in her tearfully apologizing to me (of course), stating that she meant nothing by it (of course), that she wasn't a racist (of course), and that she didn't realize she shouldn't be talking to a class of 12-year-olds about her infertility issues (ummm…OK). I had no more problems with that teacher for the remainder of the year, and her contract wasn't renewed.

Fast forward to my professional career. While on a call with a director (Black man) and another member of his team (Black woman), I was referred to as "sweetie." I thought that I misheard him the first time, until he said it again. After convincing myself to keep it cool, I professionally responded, "I would appreciate it if you please not refer to me as sweetie."

Of course, this automatically offended him, and he quickly attempted to speak over me and state, "Dr. Washington, I refer to all women as sweetie. I refer to the women in this office as sweetie." "I don't really care how you refer to any other women who work for you. First of all, I don't. Second, regardless of whether I did or they do, you are completely out of order and disrespectful for referring to any of us as such." Cue more of his raised voice and attempts to dismiss his actions and my offense. I should note that the woman on the call remained completely quiet during this entire 10-minute back and forth. I completely understood why, which was all the more reason why I refused to let it go. He wasn't my direct supervisor. He couldn't do anything to affect my job. In fact, I think he forgot that fact in the midst of the conversation. After I eventually told him the conversation was over (because what he wasn't about to do was disrespect me), I contacted a female colleague for her advice. She told me to document it and send it to the appropriate people. I did, and that problem was quickly addressed, including a prompt apology. I was pleased to learn that he also stopped inappropriately referring to women who worked for him as "sweetie."

Even now, I understand that I currently live in the South, and "sweetie" is a term of endearment for many. However, that term (in my world) is reserved for people I know or have a personal relationship with. I always remember that sixth-grade teacher and how my parents showed me, by example, that silence is acceptance. Never be afraid to fight for you. Actions have consequences, but only if you hold people accountable.

While you're holding others accountable, be sure you're holding yourself accountable as well. For example, my expectations of students in my class are simple. Late arrivals are prohibited. When in class, devices (phones and laptops) are to be used only for class-related purposes. Other uses mean that points are deducted from the total points possible in the class, no questions asked. If any student decides to leave class before it ends without prior approval, then points will also be deducted. Finally, there is no sleeping or doing other things in my class that are unrelated to the lecture or content. When providing the rationale for these expectations (which honestly shouldn't require any), I inform the class that I can't do any of these, because the complaints will roll in.

If I were to pull out my phone in the middle of class and answer a call, respond to a text, or check my social media, then again, there would be complaints about my rudeness or disrespect for the class and their tuition. As such, I ensure I always show up to class before the start time, with lecture notes loaded and any other material ready. I also ensure my ringer is turned off and only use my phone to record the lecture for students. I am more than prepared for every class with relevant discussion material and practice problems to help students understand the content. I'm accountable to my students, and in turn, I expect them to also be accountable to me. Unfortunately, neither of us can play by our own rules in class so, what's good for the goose must also be good for the gander.

Study Long, Study Wrong

If you wait too long to act on something, then you may miss your window of opportunity (which may never come again). We often are hesitant to take chances, especially as a double minority who is often marginalized in our academic and/or professional environments. It's not always the most comfortable (as we've already discussed) to step outside of our comfort zones, although we must do it in order to be successful.

I often see the hesitation of Black women and girls to take a leap of faith when it comes to their ideas and innovation. How many times have you seen an app, software, or product and thought about how you had that *exact* same idea several years earlier? You could've been rich, right? How many times have you thought about applying for that job or asking for that promotion or raise, then decided against it? What stopped you?

Our desire to have the perfect product or resume often hinders us from becoming the next big tech entrepreneur or advancing in our careers. We strive for perfection (which is great), but often slow down our trajectory. This is a short and simple chapter. One of the best ways to ensure you never miss your window of opportunity is to simply jump. Sometimes being prepared simply means taking a leap of faith. How many times will you be able to capture lightning in a bottle?

One of my college coaches always stressed the five P's: Prior preparation prevents poor performance. Again, if you stay ready, you don't have to get ready. If you have an idea, cultivate it. If you've started a project, release it. Modifications are what version control is designed for. Start small, iterate, learn, and grow. If you want that promotion, job, or raise, ask for it. Believe that you can and will, simply because you already have. Don't wait for someone else to capitalize off of your great idea or take your position.

When you do get that chance, make sure that you give yourself the fighting chance you deserve. As a consultant, I always respond to clients in less than 24 hours when contacted. This is because nothing is guaranteed. If they contacted me, then the logical assumption is that they contacted several others as well. If I want their business, then it's my responsibility to demonstrate that I'm the best person for the job by promptly and professionally responding. If I'm fortunate enough to work with them, then I always ensure that I meet deadlines and requirements. Again, they could've taken their business elsewhere. Remember, your work should precede you.

I can't tell you how many times I've tried to work with people, only to have them take days if not weeks to respond, if they responded at all. Even in working on this book, I attempted to contact several people regarding various needs. There is a lot to be said about promptness and professional courtesies, especially in business. It doesn't bode well to someone looking to do business with you that you don't respond to them in a timely manner. My money spends the same as anyone else's, so remember that when you choose to market yourself. Time and Muva wait for no one.

Fear Not Failure or Rejection: Shake That Imposter Syndrome

"Fail fast, fail often" is a popular mantra for computer scientists, especially when learning to program. However, failure and rejection are both scary and hard to view positively, especially in a field where we're already marginalized because of our gender and skin color. As Black women, we're often taught that failure is not an option. Again, the "twice-as-good" rule is so engrained in our minds that we often don't allow ourselves the chance to embrace and accept failure because, in some way, it is a reflection of our abilities and character. If I'm supposed to be twice as good as everyone else, how can I logically accept failure in any capacity? It's a tangled web, but it's one we must learn to navigate better.

First things first, we *must* stop putting the pressure and unrealistic expectation of being perfect on our shoulders. Other students and professionals in the tech field embrace failure as a chance to grow and learn. After all, build, test, improve, and iterate is how we learn to program. Why then is it so hard to translate this same practice to everywhere outside of class?

I've met young women who failed in their first attempt at a class, project, or venture and were so affected by it that their confidence was completely shaken. They convinced themselves that CS was too difficult and not for them. The problem with this is that there were so many lost lessons to be learned in those failures and so many lost innovations with their surrenders.

However, the feeling associated with that failure was permanently inked in their minds and became their rationale for how they weren't strong enough CS students.

Tackling Imposter Syndrome

Imposter syndrome describes your belief that, despite your educational and professional accomplishments, you don't belong in the current environment that you've successfully earned the right to be in. You question if you're a fraud and how long it will be before everyone else realizes it, if they haven't already. If you've never experienced imposter syndrome, then you probably know someone who has. If you've ever felt like this, then fear not. You are *far* from alone.

I completed my undergraduate studies with a 4.0 GPA. However, my first semester as a graduate student, I failed the midterm in my Parallel Architectures course. The class average was around a 65, and I scored somewhere around a 50 after the curve. I was completely devastated and imposter syndrome reared its ugly head. I immediately went into a tailspin of panic about what I was doing there, how I would make it through a Ph.D. program when I'd just failed the first exam in my first semester as a graduate student, and all of the people I would disappoint by failing out of school. I note that I can be a bit dramatic at times.

After calling my mother in a panic, she let me cry my eyes out and then said in a calm-yet-stern tone, "You accepted money from these people (my fellowships) to go to school. You have no choice but to gather yourself, figure out how to improve for the next test, and do what you need to do to pass that class." It wasn't really the most helpful advice at the time (she can be a bit of a straight shooter). However, it *did* force me to figure out a game plan. This class clearly would require above and beyond measures to get through it. The first thing I did was visit the professor during office hours, who informed me that the lectures were recorded and the VHS tapes (yes, VHS) were stored in the library. However, the library maintained only one copy for a class of 50. For the remainder of that semester, I spent at least three nights per week in the library for hours reviewing the lectures, taking additional notes, and researching additional information to help understand the course material. I was often waiting for the professor to arrive for office hours each week, and I made sure that I was well prepared with what I'd accomplished, what I understood, and where I was stuck and needed his help. By the end of the semester, I earned an 83 on the final exam, surprising even myself. I remember visiting the professor to thank him for his assistance and he informed me that he'd never seen a student do such a turnaround in his course.

In that one moment where I'd originally felt completely defeated, I could've thrown in the towel, accepted that I didn't belong in the graduate program, dropped out of school, and taken a job in industry. Instead, I used that failure as a wake up call and found a way to regroup, reset, and retry. My success didn't happen by continuing to do what I'd always done. I had to find a way to learn from my mistakes, create a game plan, and do whatever it took to improve. It meant sacrificing even more of my time, especially with friends and family. However, it was a temporary sacrifice that helped me reach a permanent goal.

While we may think that failure is not an option for us as Black women, we often need to accept it when it comes, identify the lesson, regroup, reset, and retry. Failure doesn't make you an imposter; it makes you human. No one is perfect in this field...no one. Everything won't always go as we intended, especially the first time around. Not only is that perfectly normal, it's also OK. It's still a lesson I struggle with daily. However, we have to learn that failure isn't final. It's a temporary setback that we can choose to either learn from or wallow in.

I've had the pleasure of watching several young Black women learn this same lesson over the past 13 years as a professor. Two in particular failed my programming course miserably the first time they completed it. I even suggested they drop or audit the course before the deadline and retake it the following semester, to ensure it didn't affect their GPA. Both declined and said they wanted to complete the course in full. Neither had any prior CS experience, and both were completely lost most of the time in the lectures. However the following semester, both of them were complete rock stars. They not only passed the course with an A, but also participated in class, answering questions and whiteboarding short programs to explain to their classmates. Towards the end of the semester, I asked each of them what happened. What was the game changer between the previous and current semesters? Both of them said they simply dug deep and used the summer to review all of the course material and additional information they found online to help them better understand the content. It sounded all too familiar.

Learn to View Rejection as Redirection

Just as we need to become fearless in the face of failure, the same goes for rejection. I admit, this is *still* something that I struggle with as well. After all, rejection can hurt, depending on who it comes from and how it's delivered. However, as we were often told as kids, everyone won't like you or want to play with you. That's *their* problem, not yours. It's your responsibility to not internalize that rejection, continue to be your most authentic self, and remember to persist and persevere in spite of it.

In my first year of graduate studies, I had to find an advisor willing to work with me as a graduate student. I'd carefully researched the faculty in the CS department and identified a small handful of professors who were doing research in areas of interest. The first professor I met with (the one I briefly mentioned before) was beyond arrogant and condescending. After asking me a few questions, he made it clear (in no uncertain terms) that he'd never heard of my undergraduate institution (even though it was 2.5 hours away in Charlotte), and while I may have graduated with a 4.0 GPA, he didn't think I was able to meet his research expectations. After quickly gathering myself, I politely thanked him for his time and left.

To say I was insulted is an understatement. However, I wasn't surprised. Unfortunately, at only 22 years old, I'd already encountered so many men and women like him who thought that me being a Black girl or woman automatically meant that I should be written off as less than qualified to accomplish anything comparable to them. Instead, I used that man's insulting remarks as motivation to ensure that I not only found an advisor, but also successfully completed my Ph.D. The person who became my advisor was an amazing man who taught me so much about CS as well as myself. He became my strongest ally and advocate at the university, and as his first Black graduate student, we often discussed everything from networking to how my hair grew so much when I walked in with braids (thankfully, he never asked to touch it). However, the most important thing about him was that he made me feel safe. He made it clear that his main goal was to help me graduate as quickly as possible. After all, it didn't look good for him to have seven and eight-year graduate students. He also taught me (indirectly) that rejection should be viewed as redirection. Had that first professor not rejected me, I would've never met this amazing man who literally helped me become the person I am today.

It's not always that easy to see, in the midst of rejection, how you're being redirected to something better. It often feels like a gut punch that you least expected. However, it's a part of life, and it's a part of the process. Fear of rejection is normal. However, being afraid to try is crippling both professionally and personally. We are already such a minority in this field that it's hard to feel "accepted" in many circles, be it study groups, class discussions, professional circles, and work functions. However, overcoming those fears makes us the unicorns that we are destined to become through resilience. When certain graduate classes required group work, how easy do you think it was to find other students interested in working with me, the one Black woman (or Black student period) in the course? However, I had to take the initiative and find other students to collaborate with.

I recently met a woman who told me about a software product she'd developed over a year ago. She had a few people interested in it. However, she'd never fully marketed it because she knew it had bugs and didn't have the funding to hire someone to help fix them. She assumed a larger audience would be disinterested, because of these bugs. Rather than face rejection, she tabled the product, along with her time, effort, and dream. I reminded her that Google kept Gmail in a beta phase for almost five years! Did people stop using it? Did it disappear to never be heard of again? Absolutely not!

As Black women, our fears often hinder us from throwing caution to the wind and putting ourselves (and more importantly our creations) out there for the world to see, consume, and enjoy. We have to be audacious enough to believe that everyone won't need, like, or use what we have to offer, and that's OK. Do it anyway. Create it anyway. Be it anyway. You only have one turn at this thing called life. Make sure you leave it with no regrets.

Don't Be Afraid to Ask for Help

I cannot repeat this enough: It's OK to *not* know. We often place unrealistic expectations on ourselves to have the answers for everything. This fallacy often hinders our personal and professional growth. Not a single person in this field knows everything there is to know, nor does he/she *not* rely on the assistance of others at some point. If anyone tells you otherwise, then they're lying.

I often encounter students who are completely lost in the class, yet still refuse to ask for help. Whatever they're doing in terms of studying isn't working, yet they never come to office hours, ask questions in class, or email questions after the lecture. Instead, they suffer in silence until it's too late and they either drop or fail the course. This same pattern then follows them into the professional world.

My first time visiting Turks and Caicos, I traveled alone and decided to do a snorkeling excursion. I was the only Black person on the boat, aside from the tour guides, and it was my first time snorkeling. There were probably 15 people on the excursion, and the tour guides allowed us to hang out in the water for a little longer if we wanted, including using the built-in slide on the boat. Since I can swim, I decided to ditch the life preserver and use the slide. It dumped me no more than 10-15 feet from the ladder, so no big deal, right?

I neglected the fact that I was completely out of shape at the time, I'd just spent three hours in the heat and water, and this was the ocean, not a pool. I also took for granted that the tour guides (who effortlessly and repeatedly dove into ocean water to find fresh conch for the entire boat) were in the best shape of their lives as they swam like Michael Phelps back towards the boat all day, every day. Suffice it to say I hit the water and, as soon as I started treading water, I quickly realized that I needed to get back to that ladder ASAP, as I was *much* more tired than I'd anticipated. I literally panicked and began swimming for my life. At one point, I was *just* out of arms reach of the ladder and came up for air, panicked even more, and went back underwater to swim. My logic: If I was underwater, then no one could see how exhausted (and panicked) I was. Smart move, I know. This entire ordeal probably lasted less than three minutes. However, the only thing I kept telling myself was I *cannot* drown out here. I *cannot* be the only Black person on this boat (and know how to swim) and need one of these tour guides to dive in and rescue me. I *cannot* look bad in front of these White folks.

By the time I reached the ladder (again, maybe 10-15 feet in distance), I was so exhausted that I couldn't even stand up on it. I had to take a minute and sit there on my knees until I gathered myself, then climb up the ladder, exhausted and breathing like I just finished the Boston marathon. It's something I can laugh about now with my mom and friends. However, in that moment, it was one of the scariest things I'd ever experienced. What's worse, it was *completely* self-induced. My refusal to ask for help (for fear of what it would look like as the only Black woman on the boat) could have easily killed me.

How many times have you been too afraid or stubborn to ask for help, knowing that you absolutely needed it? We're often so conditioned to be the "fixer," to have the solution to all of our problems (and at least half of everyone else's) that we see asking for help as a sign of weakness. The strongest people are those who acknowledge they can't do it all and need others. Your strength lies in knowing that you can't go it alone, be it school, work, or life.

I have to insert a disclaimer here as well. Should you ask for help, make sure you've taken the necessary steps to prepare yourself as much as possible. My students know that they can never tell me in a lab or office hours "I don't know how to do this." That is an insufficient statement. I expect them to show me what they've done, where they're stuck, and what they think is hindering them from moving forward. When asking for help, people are more inclined to provide it when they see you've done some of the legwork. Remember my first-semester failure as a graduate student? This goes for your career as well. You will often find that you need assistance from colleagues or collaborators. That's perfectly OK. However, please ensure you've done some research on the problem and can articulate what you've done and where you're stuck. You'll be amazed at how often people will be willing to help you. You'll also learn quickly to work smarter not harder.

Somehow and somewhere many of us became afraid of asking for the help we need. That myth of being the strong Black woman that can "fix" everything and doesn't need anyone's help often hinders us more than we realize. We'd rather drown than yell for someone to throw us a life preserver, simply because of how it looks to others (who in the grand scheme of things, don't matter at all). If you gain nothing else from this chapter and my story, remember that your true strength is in knowing when to ask for the help you need and deserve.

Keep Receipts

This is probably one of the easier pieces of free jewelry to offer. Document everything. If there are issues with a professor, colleague, supervisor, or peer, then document it. Proper documentation of events and conversations is often one of the easiest ways to support your case when situations arise. Let's be honest. Things happen, the truth gets cloudy, and it can often come down to your word against someone else's. You never want to be in a situation where you don't have evidence to support your stance.

One semester, a colleague made an inappropriate comment to me at a work-related event. I could have easily called her on it at that moment. However, I didn't think it was the most appropriate time to address it. Besides, I needed to process what happened before responding. Instead, I gave myself until the following morning to see if I still felt strongly about it. I did, and therefore documented the event with the appropriate personnel to ensure a few things: 1)The incident was appropriately documented; 2)it was accurate and professionally expressed my displeasure and offense; and 3)should there be any future interactions with this colleague, there was already documentation showing that I'd expressed prior concerns.

Even if you don't submit the information to anyone, it is still important to immediately and properly document the date, time, and incident for your own records. You never know what future events may occur that require supporting evidence to show a pattern. Email exchanges are a perfect way to preserve documentation of conversations and agreements. I often tell students and professionals to keep all correspondence written, if possible. This ensures that things never become your word against someone else's. In addition, it provides an accurate timestamp. Even if things are discussed in person, always follow up with an email confirming the conversation.

Second, always remember to remain professional. It's very easy for people to label us as angry or confrontational when we're simply being direct, assertive, or justifiably defending ourselves. As hard as it may be at times (and trust me, I know *just* how hard that is), do your best to remain professional and factual. Save the venting for your tribe or close confidants.

I was in my fourth year of graduate school when I needed to obtain all of the paystubs associated with my graduate stipends from the university. For some reason, I'd stop receiving them via mail because I moved. I called the appropriate campus office to inform them and was greeted by one of the rudest women I'd ever spoken to. She informed me that not only was it not the office's responsibility to get these to me, but they didn't even have them. I informed her that, over the past four years, these same stubs were mailed to me quarterly from the same office, so I wasn't sure how all of a sudden they were no longer there. She quickly informed me that wasn't her issue and she had other things to worry about before rudely ending the call.

I could have cursed that lady out or visited her office the next day just to keep the "conversation" going. However, I wasn't about to waste precious gas and time driving to campus to deal with that woman again. I took a moment to calm down, then found her email address (as well as her director's) on the university website. That evening, I sent a professional email to the director detailing the entire conversation with this woman, why I originally requested the information, how this was not out of the ordinary (as it was the standard university procedure for the past few years), and how I did not appreciate the lack of professionalism or courtesy I was afforded as a Ph.D. student, especially since my fellowships were external to the university. I also made sure to CC that woman.

The next evening, I had a knock on my door at approximately 7 p.m. Assuming it was one of my parents stopping by, I opened the door and was shocked to see a woman I'd never met before who was almost in tears. It wasn't until I saw a stack of paystubs in her hand that I realized it was the same woman who was completely rude to me on the phone the previous day. She asked if I was Alicia Washington (yes), then introduced herself and quickly added, "I want to say that I am *SO* very sorry for how I spoke to you yesterday. It was completely wrong and rude and I am so sorry." I think I was still so shocked that this woman was standing at my doorstep that all I could respond with was "OK. Thanks." I'll never know what her director said to her. Whatever it was, it was serious enough for this woman to get in her car...after work...with her kids in the car...and drive the 25 minutes from NC State's campus to my house in Durham to personally deliver those paystubs (NOT checks...paystubs) at 7 p.m.

This is why I say always keep receipts. I've spoken to students who don't feel like they have a voice, because they are students going against faculty, staff, or administrators. I've also spoken with colleagues across other institutions who have faced issues with coworkers, administrators, students, and even parents. My first piece of advice is to always document everything. My second is to determine if it's worth escalating, and if so, determine the appropriate point of contact. If you choose this route, remember to hold everyone accountable. There's now a paper trail that includes anyone who was notified. If they don't respond within a reasonable time or with an acceptable resolution, then you must decide whether to further escalate it. Remember to pick your battles wisely. Every hill isn't worth dying on. However, if you do feel that certain, then definitely push forward. No one will fight for you like you will.

Stay Current

The tech field is constantly changing and evolving. There are technologies we have yet to create that will completely disrupt our daily lives in the next five to ten years. Given the level of underrepresentation of Black women, we must stay current in order to stay relevant and competitive. We cannot afford to be stagnant, or we risk being left behind in the next tech revolution.

There are so many resources available and opportunities to explore, that it can be hard to determine where to start. The answer is simple: Choose something and continue from there. Subscribe to and follow technical blogs, websites, magazines, and articles to learn what the current and consistent trends are. Then identify resources that can help you develop these skill sets. This can include books, courses, and online training. It's always a good idea to continue to refine your programming skills, including learning a new language. Most CS graduates learn JAVA, C/C++, and/or Python. Use these foundational languages to learn a new one.

One of the things to remember as you develop or refine your programming skills is that no one knows everything there is to know about any language. Yes, there are individuals who are more experienced. However, as I tell my students, good programmers are simply good designers. They had a great design, knew where to find the syntax to map to it, and further developed their skills from there. They leveraged books, application programming interfaces (APIs), and websites to accomplish their goals.

In the age of the Internet, you can find plenty of online courses that are free and self-paced on just about any topic you can think of. Take advantage of these. Many cities also have meetup groups that include other developers interested in not only connecting with developers around the city, but also further improving their skills. Don't be afraid to take advantage of these opportunities. Remember, part of your success is built on the connections you make. If you're a student, take advantage of some of those elective courses in your department.

Finally, I encourage each of you to tinker outside of work or classes. What you do in the classroom or on the job will never be enough to keep you as current as you need to be. Take extra time each day or week to create something. It doesn't have to be anything large. The key is you're further developing your technical skills and also building a portfolio that can be used to introduce your newest product, showcase to potential employers, or build the foundation of your entrepreneurial ventures.

Write, Write, Write

One of the best ways to set yourself apart in this field is to perfect your writing skills. It may seem like it isn't a big deal, and many of you may prefer not to write. However, you should consider it a necessary evil that can help you get further ahead. If you think about it, most tech people hate to write anything. Developers create programs. However, many don't want to take the time to document them and explain their use. In addition, in a field where so much work is still outsourced, many companies want documentation of their products by individuals who fully understand the technical aspects of the product, can explain it to novices and experts in a clear and concise manner, and speak English as a native language.

This provides opportunities to create technical documentation such as website content, blog articles, APIs, and user guides. If you choose to pursue a graduate degree or career in academia, then your writing skills will either make or break you. You will have to create course materials, proposals, technical papers, and more. How will you be successful in any of these endeavors if you can't write well?

Remember what I discussed about being twice as good? If you currently have or are completing a college or advanced degree, then your professional communication skills should reflect that. I confess that I hated writing in high school. However, my English teachers required so many argumentative essays that I had to develop those skills in order to reduce the red ink on my papers. As I matriculated in college, the same applied. I assumed majoring in CS would require little, if any, writing. However, attending a liberal arts university and being a part of the Honors College meant that I had to write much more than I expected. Thankfully, once again, all of my professors were heavy with a red pen and critiqued my papers so much that, by the time I began working with my advisor as a graduate student, he was quite impressed with my writing skills.

However, my biggest challenge (aside from the research) as a graduate student was learning how to become a technical writer. From grades K-16, we're taught to write argumentatively: Choose a position, provide evidence to support it, and conclude such that you reiterate your overarching argument. This writing style doesn't work for technical writing. No one wants to read fluff or filler material. Everything must be clear and concise with only facts. Readers want to know the purpose of the study, related literature, novelty of the proposed work, methodology used, results obtained, and future work (if any). It took significant practice (and a ton of red ink on my advisor's part) to finally reach a point where my technical writing skills were strong. I'm grateful that he provided me a number of opportunities to develop these skills, well before my first technical manuscript was submitted to a journal or conference.

Just like any other art form, writing requires practice. To become great, you must be willing to work on developing those skills repeatedly and accept harsh criticism. The best way to develop your writing skills is to read everything, including books, technical papers, blog articles, and web content. In addition, continue to read newspapers and other non-technical documents that help you further develop your vocabulary. For everything you create, document it. If you read a technical paper, write a one or two-paragraph summary of it. If you create a website or product, write a short blurb about it. The only way to become better at something is to continuously practice it. In addition, share your work with others for constructive criticism. Most importantly, accept the criticism as just that: constructive. It may be hard to receive when your work is filled with red ink or suggested edits via Track Changes. However, use that as a baseline. Aim for less red marks with each iteration until you have little to no edits to complete. This is when you know you've become a much better writer.

Finally, once you find yourself comfortable as a writer, never stop working on these skills. There are opportunities that pay just as well as the best software developers to document the same programs being created. After all, how many people can read, create, understand, and discuss programs? You may find additional opportunities to venture outside of the normal technical writing space as well. After all, you *are* reading this book, right?

Take Time to Celebrate You

We often get so caught up in all of the things we still have to complete that we don't stop and recognize all of the things we've already accomplished. I'm guilty of doing this more often than not. There are only so many hours in a day and so many things to do that I only consider completion of a "big ticket item" a major accomplishment.

I'm an avid list creator. Every day, I create a to-do list of things to complete. As a task is completed, I cross it out. If something remains incomplete, then it gets transferred to the next day's list. Some things have been transferred for the past month or two. Others get knocked out in a matter of 30 minutes to one hour. It's just my thing. If I don't have a list (on paper, because I need to physically be able to cross that item out), then I'm mentally all over the place. Even though I *know* what I'm supposed to get done, it's almost impossible for me to get a good handle on anything without a list. At least I can tackle the small items first, which may be as simple as paying a bill or scheduling a doctor's appointment. Other larger items include writing two more chapters of this book (for example), grading a quiz or homework assignment, updating my CV, or reviewing and preparing for a class lecture. There's something about the validation of looking at a piece of paper and seeing things crossed off that motivates me.

Having said that, this type of list forces me to always focus on the *next* task to complete. At the end of each day, I can honestly say I hardly ever take a moment to recognize all that I've accomplished. I usually have so many irons in the fire that it's hard to see a success as anything other than a fully completed list. I admit that this isn't always the most productive way to work. Hence, this chapter is just as much advice for myself as it is for each of you reading it.

After completing my master's degree, I didn't even participate in graduation. I finished in August of 2002 and immediately moved into my Ph.D. work with my advisor. Once I completed my Ph.D., I spent the summer focused on finding a place to live in Washington, DC, selling my place in Durham, and preparing for my transition from graduate student to working professional. When I left The Aerospace Corporation, my last day was on a Friday. I started my first class at Howard the following Monday.

When I earned tenure and promotion, I pushed right on with the next set of tasks I needed to accomplish. When I left Howard for Winthrop, I spent the entire summer closing out things in DC and preparing for my relocation to Charlotte. Even this summer, after receiving notification that a manuscript was accepted for publication in a journal, I instantly crossed that major item off my to-do list and moved on to the next task.

The problem with this type of list is that it's never fully completed. There's always something transferred or added to the next day. At what point do you stop to celebrate the fact that five small (but important) tasks were accomplished, when that one major task still remains? We often focus on the major victories that we miss the time we should be taking to stop, breathe, and reflect on the small ones as motivation to push forward.

Even if it's something small, do something to recognize what you *have* done, instead of staying so focused on what you still have outstanding. This could be as simple as taking a study break, treating yourself to dinner or dessert, or taking a moment to just veg out and do nothing. Stop and smell the roses.

Comfort Breeds Complacency

There's no room for getting comfortable in this field. As we previously discussed, everything evolves so rapidly that you can easily get left behind. As Black women and girls in the tech field, it's important that we continue growing, expanding, and pushing ourselves to achieve new goals.

I often tell my students to be present and *be* present. This may seem redundant, but it's far from it. The first "be present" means to actually be in attendance. Go to class, attend the meetings, and be on time. The second "be present" means to be fully engaged in what you're supposed to be doing. If it's class, then be fully engaged in the discussion, asking and answering questions, taking notes, and interacting with the professor and classmates as appropriate. If it's work, then immerse yourself in the project or task, including collaborating with colleagues as necessary. Eliminate distractions such as phones, social media, texts, or conversations that are not directly related to the work. You'd be surprised at how much more productive you can actually be (typed as I alternate between Instagram and this chapter). Like I said, I'm a work in progress, and some of this is just as much for me as it is for you.

The other thing I tell students is to show up and show out. Make yourself known for the *right* reasons. At the beginning of every semester, I tell each class that if I don't know them by name by the time midterm exams are returned, then they aren't doing something right. The students I remember are the ones who consistently engage, asking questions, participating in class, and

73

volunteering to whiteboard program solutions. They're the students who aren't afraid to be wrong or not know, but are more concerned with fully understanding the material. They come to office hours prepared with what they've done, where they're stuck, and what their concerns are. These are the students I remember when I get a call or email asking me to identify someone for a scholarship or internship. These are the students (or employees) you should always choose to be.

You never know who someone knows or what opportunities they may be able to expose you to. This is why you should never remain in your comfort zone. It's very easy to fly under the radar in class or at work. You'd rather not ruffle feathers, be bothered with answering a question, or interact with that annoying colleague. Comfort zones are safe havens, but they also are where dreams go to die. When you become comfortable, you often become stagnant. There is no desire to move forward or stretch yourself, because this requires a level of discomfort that you're either not used to or have no desire to experience.

Think about the last time you were seated in an uncomfortable position. As I type, I'm currently seated in a library in New York City that is *unbelievably* cold. Given that I only have on a tank top and shorts, I'm freezing. 1 can't sit still, because I'm too cold. I have to keep readjusting in my seat and moving to eliminate some level of discomfort. However, if it were too comfortable in here (because they turned the thermostat up to make it a little warmer), I would end up asleep and unproductive. This discomfort keeps me awake, alert, and focused on the task I need to complete.

The same logic can be applied to the discomfort you feel in the classroom or office. It keeps you moving forward. If you're too comfortable, then you're not learning or growing. Athletes (the top ones, at least) never train to their level of comfort. They push themselves to keep going, even when they're tired. That's what makes the greatest athletes so much better than their competition. They are constantly pushing themselves to do more, which in turn makes them prepared for any competition.

The next time your teacher or professor asks for a volunteer to answer a question (or your manager asks for someone to assist with a new project), don't quickly cower behind the crowd and wait for someone else to step up. Take the lead, make yourself known, show up, and show out! Your future self will thank you for it!

Take Care of Yourself

I cannot stress enough how important your physical, mental, and emotional health are to your success. You can't truly be your best self if you aren't well in all of these areas. We live (and ultimately die) by the stigma of being a "strong Black woman." We are supposed to endure pain, heartache, stress, and suffering (with a straight face or smile), all while continuing to be everything to everyone. If there's anything wrong with us, then we're expected to suck it up, pray it away, and persist.

That's absurd.

There's so much recent literature and discussions around Black women and their physical, mental, and emotional health, and I'm *so* glad it's happening. Part of being your greatest advocate and unapologetically dope is to realize that it *is* OK to *not* be OK! We're human. We get tired, overwhelmed, hurt, and upset. We laugh, cry, scream, and shout. It doesn't make us any less than or weaker because, at any given time, we aren't our best selves. What's important is that, in those moments where we are less than our best, we identify and use the resources available to help get us back to where we need to be.

Mental and Emotional Health

One of the biggest stigmas in the Black community is that mental health isn't a thing. How many times have you heard (or read) someone say that all a person needs is a little prayer and positive thinking? If only it were that easy. There is *nothing* wrong

77

with being concerned about and taking care of your mental health. There is *nothing* wrong with having mental health challenges. More people than you know have suffered from some sort of challenge at some point in their lives. Until we, as a community, stop placing a negative stigma on it, then we will continue to see one too many of our own suffering from the effects of poor mental health.

In May of 2013, my father had surgery to remove what we thought was one spot around his stomach. After surgery, the doctor informed my mother and me that there were so many other spots found that he could only remove what he could see. The prognosis wasn't good. At 35 years old, I was facing the fact that my father wouldn't be around to walk me down the aisle, meet his grandchild, or witness all of these other things in life that I had yet to accomplish. I spent the next two months literally in my father's hospital room in North Carolina, watching the man who'd been my first everything become unable to even wipe drool from his own mouth, and I didn't know how to deal with that.

On top of this, I had a professional development program for 20 K-12 teachers to prepare for in DC and three graduate students whose financial aid and stipends I was responsible for ensuring were appropriately processed before August. To say I was all over the place is an understatement. My father died on July 22 (the first day of my program), two days after he told me to go home and get ready for it, and one day after he called me and said he was tired, begged me to let him go, and made me promise him I'd be OK. I was literally sitting in my department chair's office when his office phone rang and he recognized the 919 area code. It was my mom, in tears. I had zero time to properly grieve my father's death. I tried to finish the day, go home, pack, and drive home. I stayed in North

Carolina until the day before classes started in mid-August and went right back into the swing of things. By November, I completely spiraled and had a breakdown on my living room floor. Thankfully, one of my girlfriends (and tribe members) came to my house, sat with me, and ensured my mom she would stay with me through the night.

Only a handful of my closest friends ever knew that story…until now. I kept going, first in May while sitting in the hospital daily on my computer or phone, trying to ensure financial aid paperwork was processed and other information was received. Next, it was while I was back in DC and trying to get through the first day of the program knowing my father had just passed away and my phone was being flooded with calls and texts. The next was after his funeral, when I had just enough time to inhale and get ready for the fall semester, classes, and research. It was inevitable that I cracked. It took therapy, antidepressants, and the end of a relationship to finally (and properly) grieve my father's death and be OK. There isn't a day that goes by that I don't miss or think about him, and some days I end up emotional just hearing a song he loved. However, the one thing I've learned is that's OK. More importantly, I'm OK.

My graduate advisor was an avid sailor, so much so that he would take a week or two during each semester (and several times over the summer) to sail. The first time he did this, he informed me that he would be unavailable for two weeks, with no access to a computer or phone (except for emergency purposes). Anything I needed in that time would have to wait until he returned. You can imagine the anxiety that filled my entire body upon receiving this news. What happened if something went wrong with my research or I needed help? How was I supposed to continue working while this man is off sailing up and down the East Coast? Why was he not as concerned about any of this as I was? How *dare* he just disappear for two weeks while I'm knee deep in this program!

I didn't understand it at the time, but this was my advisor's way of decompressing. It was his way of ensuring that he maintained his mental and emotional health by visiting his "happy place," which helped him regroup and reset. One of the best pieces of advice he gave me after his first return (and my subsequent brain dump of how high my anxiety had been for that entire two-week period) was that completing a Ph.D. was less about the research and more about learning yourself: how you work best, how you handle failure, and what you need to do whenever you've lost focus. For him, it was sailing. I didn't realize how important this advice was until I became a college professor myself. After losing my father (and doing my work), I learned that when I feel those moments of anxiety coming (where everything is happening and I feel overwhelmed), I have to stop. It may be for one day or one week. Whatever that time is, I detach completely. I may watch television, work out, or take a quick road trip. Whatever it is, I don't touch anything work-related until that time is up.

I've also designated one day each week as my personal "mental health day." I don't do any work-related things (no emails, no work, nothing). I clean my house, work out, treat myself to lunch, a movie, a pedicure, or massage, and simply exist. Whatever I choose to do on Saturday or Sunday is my call. However, that *one* day each week during the academic year helps me to regroup and reset. While I recognize that everyone doesn't have the flexibility in their schedules to designate a weekly mental health day, you absolutely *must* find whatever methods help you to decompress in those moments when you feel the most overwhelmed and anxious.

Your emotional health should complement your mental health to ensure that you're able to deal with stress, anxiety, depression, doubt, and more. This includes how you handle adversity and thinking before you act (or speak), for example. Are you able to remain emotionally stable when challenges arise? As a disclaimer, my degrees are in CS, so I don't claim to be an expert on *any* of this. However, I see a lot more young people who are facing personal challenges that I couldn't imagine at their age. These can't help but affect their mental health, which can't help but affect everything else. I can only share my story with you, in hopes that it will help you learn from my experiences. As a wise woman once told me, "Sometimes you don't have to get burned to know there's a fire."

Allowing myself to feel what I feel in that moment and move through it has been so much better for me than trying to suppress it and "push on" because I have a ton of things to do and people depending on me. I learned a hard lesson that I share with women all the time: If you die tomorrow, the only questions will be "Why didn't she leave us her passwords? Where are her keys? Who can finish this work for us?" That's it. So stop killing yourself to please others and focus more on yourself. You only have *one* shot at this thing called life. Be good to yourself.

Physical Health

While we are making sure that we are OK mentally and emotionally, it's equally important to make sure that we're OK physically. Stress is killing so many Black women and can lead to so many other health issues that we never know about until it's too late. Exercise at least a few times per week. Even 30 minutes per day can go a long way for your physical (and mental) health. I grew up running track and playing basketball. However, the way my knees are set up, I can no longer do either. I therefore have to do cardio that keeps me motivated and engaged, such as boxing (cause who doesn't like to punch something), running in a pool, or using elliptical machines.

In addition to exercise, drink plenty of water and maintain healthy eating habits. I confess, I *love* to eat (bread and potatoes, especially). I'm convinced I could successfully live on those two alone. However, everything in moderation. Eat plenty of fruits and vegetables (the more colors the better). Given the fact that most of us will spend a large amount of time in front of a computer (sitting or standing at a desk), then make sure you have an ergonomically correct workspace, including your chair, desk, and keyboard. Trust me, all of this will matter 10-20 years from now, and your body will thank you, one way or another.

Finally, make sure you pay attention to your body. You know it better than anyone else. Get regular checkups and be sure to visit the doctor when something isn't right. If you aren't comfortable with the diagnosis provided, then speak up for yourself. Even Serena Williams documented how she had to fight to properly diagnose her own illness following childbirth (which saved her life), because her doctors refused to believe that she knew what she was talking about. Never take what others tell you as the final decision, especially if you question its accuracy. Remember, always fight for you, because no one else will otherwise.

If there's nothing else that you gain from this chapter, I hope you remember to take care of you first. We often wear so many hats and are so many things to so many people in a single day that, we often forget that if we aren't whole, we can never truly be any good to anyone else. We are dying to be the mythological strong Black woman when we don't need to be. Having true strength is knowing when you have little to none. Take care of yourself, sis.

Never Lose Yourself

As Black women in the tech field, we often have to balance being our most authentic self with successfully navigating our work or educational environments. This fine line we walk daily can take its toll on even the best of us. While we all know there's an element of shifting we must often do to dispel the myth of the "angry Black woman," you must find a way to still remain true to yourself.

Master the Art of Code Switching

Let me be explicitly clear before someone complains. I am, in *no way*, advising you to be anything other than your most authentic self. What I *am* saying is that you must learn *how* to be that woman in any and every situation to get what you want. That woman requires adjusting to people, places, and situations. However, at her core, she remains the same. Some people call this code switching, while others call it shifting. Ultimately, it's about discovering who you are and who you need to be when you need to be her. Those who are closest to me know that there are three versions of me: Dr. Washington, Nicki, and Nick. All are authentic and unapologetic versions of me. However, the environment, crowd, and my level of comfort dictate who I am at any moment.

Dr. Washington is the professional. You'll see her at work interacting with students, faculty, staff, and administrators, or other professional settings where she's introduced with a title. Her words and actions are very intentional, because she realizes that, despite her educational and professional achievements, certain people will still question her abilities. Consequently, she's learned which battles are worth fighting and is willing to die on those hills. She's also developed a thick skin and quick wit that allows her to handle any situation in the most professional-yet-direct manner possible.

Nicki is the person most people meet in casual settings. She doesn't possess an iota of a concern about titles and prefers to not discuss work, unless it's in relation to a potential collaboration or opportunity. She approaches most people with cautious optimism and will usually decide within 5-10 minutes of meeting you if she feels like entertaining any further conversation. If she doesn't, then you'll know immediately.

Nick is the unfiltered, uncut version of my most authentic self. Only those in my circle of trust get to see *that* chick. She's a little extra, a little high strung, but a *lot* of fun. She's completely loyal and will give you her last. However, she's also somewhat sensitive, so if you betray that loyalty, then it *really* sucks to be you. She always knows *what* to say and *whether* to say it or not. More often than not, she just doesn't care either way, so she says whatever she feels at the moment. Like most of us, she's clearly a work in progress.

No matter what capacity or setting you know or meet me in, there's a little bit of all three of these women in every version. The difference is understanding who to be and when to be her. For example, when my colleague made that inappropriate comment to me at work, how Nicki (or even worse Nick) would've responded would've probably lost Dr. Washington her job. However, I've learned over the years to leverage Dr. Washington's professionalism and wit to express Nicki or Nick's thoughts in a manner that drives the point home while maintaining my composure. As a disclaimer, no matter how professional and composed you remain, in some instances, you will *still* be viewed as an angry Black woman. That's their problem though, not yours.

Lift While You Climb

I've said it before and I'll continue to say it until the day I die: None of us are here by our own merits. That's not to say we haven't earned any success we've achieved. I was fortunate enough to be blessed with certain gifts. However, I also recognize that I was surrounded by a village that helped me to further cultivate them. We all stand on the shoulders of those who came before us. There are countless Black men and women who made it easier for us to navigate in this world, where we are often overlooked, spoken over, and ignored. We don't know all of their names, because they were the people like my mother and her friends, who spent entire careers at IBM, moving into the ranks of management and ensuring that their summer interns were always HBCU students. They purposely volunteered to represent IBM at career fairs on HBCU campuses across the country, recruiting students and showing them that there were Blacks in the tech field who wanted them to succeed and would properly groom them for successfully navigating corporate America.

These are the unsung heroes who will never get a movie made about them or any major recognition across the country. However, their work was no less relevant and necessary. They understood that, as daughters and sons of the Civil Rights Movement, they had a responsibility to make the path easier for their sons, daughters, and generations after them. Likewise, we all have the same responsibility to ensure that we make the path easier for those coming behind us.

My parents and friends' parents were alumni of HBCUs who built their careers as engineers, programmers, scientists, college professors, K-12 educators and administrators, attorneys, and entrepreneurs. They raised us to believe that the sky was the limit, that college was an expectation (not an option), and that we could do and be anything we put our minds to. They held us all to high standards and were unafraid to chastise us if they caught any of us performing in any way that was less than acceptable. We knew we could be anything we desired, because we saw each of them achieving their dreams. It's no surprise how many of us grew up to become doctors, professors, K-12 educators, entrepreneurs, scientists, attorneys, and more. The seeds were planted and watered long before we ever realized it.

Unfortunately, I always knew this wasn't *every* Black girl's story growing up (even in Durham). I didn't realize just how exceptional this village was until I entered college. Since then, I've tried to ensure that I participate in activities that expose as many Black students (especially girls and young women) to computing as possible. Much of my current research focuses on the use of culturally relevant pedagogy to not only expose students to CS, but more importantly retain them in the K-16 CS pipeline.

There are a number of national efforts designed to expose more students to CS, which is great. However, students have to *see* it before they can *be* it. In 2011, I led an effort to teach a year-long CS course for 120 Black and Latino students (grades 6-8) at the Howard University Middle School of Math and Science. This work was sponsored by Google, and was designed to teach students CS fundamentals through culturally relevant pedagogy, including an all-Black and Latino team of instructors that included myself, my department chair, two graduate students, and two undergraduates. We developed and implemented a full CS curriculum over that academic year, which included guest speakers of color as well. Shout out to ALL of my middle-school educators. Y'all are the REAL MVPs!

On the first day of class, we asked students to name any computer scientists they could think of. Again, there was a six-person team of instructors (all Black and Latino computer scientists) in front of them. However, the only people named were Steve Jobs (because he'd recently passed), Mark Zuckerberg, and Bill Gates. Three white men were the only computer scientists these babies could name. Yet each and every one of them was a daily consumer of technology created by CS. They still couldn't see themselves, even though they had representation literally standing in front of them. We had work to do.

Over the course of that year, we made sure that cultural relevance was the focal point of every lesson. This didn't mean we focused on things that applied to Black and Latino culture. Instead, we used what was a part of every student's daily life to teach CS fundamentals. This meant using discussions of the family member who was responsible for cooking, purchasing food, paying bills, and getting them dressed and to school on time to understand operating systems. Since most of the students used the Washington, DC metro to travel to and from school, this was used to discuss networking, specifically links, nodes, routers, and switches. When students learned HTML and created mobile apps, they were tasked with creating a website or app that could be used by students in the school or residents in their neighborhood, ward, or across the District. They were even tasked with identifying at least 20 Black and Latino computer scientists across the world.

By the end of the course, students could easily name Dr. Mark Dean, Dr. Marc Hannah, Dr. Valerie Taylor, and Dr. Richard Tapia instead of Jobs, Gates, and Zuckerberg. In addition, they reported being excited about CS, realizing there were so many opportunities for them to explore, and having interest in taking more courses in the future. We'd changed the narrative for them over the course of that academic year by intentionally and purposefully showing them images of themselves, what they loved to do, and what they were already doing in CS, so much so that it became natural for them to think of the CS context in many of their daily activities.

In a field like computing (where we are grossly underrepresented), it's imperative that we all continue to lift while we climb. None of us have fully "made it." Some of us have come a long way, but there's still much work to be done. In almost every group of students I speak to, when asked to name computer scientists, the same names always appear: Zuckerberg, Jobs, Bezos, and Gates. White men are still the status quo for one too many students. The only way that begins to change is if more of us are in front of them, showing them that we look like them and are successful in school and our careers. We don't all wear business suits or Birkenstocks. We rock cornrows, dreads, relaxers, fades, afros, and braids. We show up in stilettos or sneakers. We love hip hop, house, dancehall, trap, and R&B music. The key is that we *must* show more young people that we are just like them. By making ourselves relatable, we also make CS more relatable.

If you haven't yet found an outlet to give back in the field, then I encourage you to actively seek these out. You can research computing-based non-profit organizations in your area, local K-12 schools, or create your own event to help promote CS to students of color. There's no excuse for any of us to *not* be someone else's role model. In fact, it's our obligation. Remember, to whom much is given, much is required.

There's Enough Food at the Table for Everyone to Eat

Listen. You are NOT the first, and you will certainly NOT be the last to experience and achieve what you have or will. While we are still dismally underrepresented in this field, it's important to remember that you *do* have a sisterhood that is growing in number each day. However (like in so many other situations), there are always people who subscribe to a scarcity mentality.

What do I mean by a scarcity mentality? It's the belief some people have that there aren't enough resources, power, opportunities, or praise for everyone to have their fair share. As a result, they work hard to ensure that they are the only one to have it. These are the people who want or need to be the ONLY one doing something. You've met them before. They're the people who don't want to work with you in the study group, for fear that you'll take some of the credit. They may even be the coworkers who know they'd get further by working with you, yet they'd still rather go it alone to avoid sharing the spotlight.

If you don't think there are any of us, of you, out there who subscribe to this theory, then allow me to enlighten you. You usually find out about them at the most unexpected moment. If you fall into this category, then I urge you to take a moment to do some serious soul searching and check yourself. Unfortunately, too many of us are still the first Black woman in a number of our environments, be it graduate programs and careers. This means that you have a responsibility to kick that door wide open for all of the Black women and girls coming behind you, not close the door and turn the lock, so that you get to bask in all the glory of being "the chosen one."

I had my own encounter with this when trying to work with someone several years ago. When emailing her that I'd love to see if there were any ways in which we could collaborate, I received a response that equated to "Oh yeah? OK." Let's just say she would've been better off not responding at all than providing that. After receiving that response, I quickly realized who I was dealing with and moved on. What I won't do is beg anyone to work with me. Our circle is too small and we should all be looking to leverage each other's talents to be greater as a whole. If we all have the same goal, then we either win together or lose together.

We cannot afford to have this scarcity mindset. I repeat, we *cannot* afford to have this scarcity mindset. There are already so many barriers placed in front of us as Black women that we do ourselves a disservice by placing even more there. There is more than enough room at the table for everyone to eat, sis. How can you effectively lift while climbing when you're not even willing to work with others who look like you to advance our cause? Malcolm X said, "The most disrespected person in America is the Black woman. The most unprotected person in America is the Black woman." We are battling against the world every day that we wake up. How can you expect people who *aren't* Black women to open more doors for us when you aren't willing to hold those doors open for your fellow sisters?

Let me also clarify that I'm not referring to slackers. There are always people who want all of the glory but put in none of the work to get there. They are the group members who do minimal (if any) work, yet want the A they didn't earn on the group project, or the coworker who always seems to be busy when it's time to meet or do the heavy lifting. However, when it's game day and all eyes are on you, they're ready with a smile to discuss how challenging the work was. Don't be those people. If anything, I advocate calling those people on their slackness and holding them accountable (we already discussed this, remember). Those aren't the ones I'm referring to. There are plenty of women who are willing and able to roll their sleeves up and get their hands dirty with you. You always want to keep those people around. They are your tribe, and you'll go far collectively.

Fortunately, I've had the extreme pleasure of meeting numerous Black women in this space who are some of the most amazingly talented, gracious, humble, and down-to-earth people you would ever meet. We met years ago and have cultivated not only professional relationships, but more importantly friendships. It's beautiful to watch each other glow up and feel nothing but pride, not intimidation, jealousy, or insecurity. We understood when we all met that we were all uniquely the same and that we *needed* each other in order to grow professionally (and sometimes personally).

Think about it, who else can better understand you than you? We all tie our hair up at night, enjoy the same shows and music, and understand the importance of coconut oil, shea butter, and black soap. We can seamlessly transition from discussing our trials of being a Black woman in computing to the challenges of finding a new hairdresser. We bounce ideas off of each other and look for ways to collaborate, not isolate. This is why it's important to remember that everyone can eat. You don't have to steal the spotlight to still shine.

Own and Trust Your Dopeness

So what do you do with all this free jewelry you received in this book? You trust the fact that you *are* truly a dope young woman and you unapologetically *own* it! You've made it this far on your talent, perseverance, faith, and support. You are *not* here by accident. Think of how many of your friends and peers didn't make it to where you are right now, both academically and professionally? Trust that you're exactly where you should be, and you'll get to where you need to be, as long as you devise a plan, continue to sharpen your skills, never get comfortable, find a dope tribe, and most importantly, persist.

I've read a ton of articles on the difference between how men and women discuss their academic and professional achievements. How many times have you met a man who was bold and confident, even if he was simply loud and wrong? He was committed and unafraid to tell anyone how amazing he was (even if he really wasn't). How many times have you met a woman who downplayed herself? If congratulations were in order for a job well done, she often minimized it with, "It really wasn't that big of a deal. Anyone could've done it. I actually had a lot of help from others." Meanwhile, the same congratulations to the opposite sex was often met with, "Thanks, I worked hard" and "Yeah, I'm pretty awesome."

We as women, as *Black* women, must remember that we are just as amazing and awesome too. More importantly, we must learn to let others know just how dope we really are. Think of how many times you've been doubted by colleagues, professors, or classmates. Were they wrong about you? Did you stand up for yourself and prove them wrong? If you didn't, then why not?

This may sound like you need to become a little arrogant, and that's because you should, in moderation. Humility is a wonderful thing to have and will often allow you to build more relationships than arrogance will. While you should definitely carry yourself like the amazing and unapologetically dope woman you are, remember that you also need to create and maintain relationships with others. Don't ever get so full of yourself that you forget that. There's a fine line between confidence and arrogance. Always lean towards confidence.

For the longest time after I finished graduate school (and even now, sometimes), I would absolutely despise being introduced as "Dr. Washington" by my friends. My degrees and career were not what defined me, and it made me slightly uncomfortable to see the look of surprise on people's faces when they learned this about me. When I mentioned this to some of my friends, they responded, "You *earned* the right to be called Dr. Washington. That's not something that happens every day. We're proud of you. *You* should be proud of you too!"

It wasn't until that moment of clarity that I gave myself permission to be proud, bold, and unapologetically dope. I realized just how much of a disservice I was doing to myself. While I never wanted to feel like I was above anyone else, I never meant to inadvertently downgrade my accomplishments. Standing out didn't seem as comfortable then, even though I'd put my blood, sweat, and literal tears into earning those degrees. I had to learn to stop hiding from my spotlight and boldly step into and embrace it. Even now, 13 years later, I still catch myself getting a little uncomfortable when introduced as "Dr. Washington" in certain circles. However, if I don't toot my own horn, then how can I expect anyone else to?

You know so much more than you think you do, and you're so much more amazing than you probably realize. We're taught to stay humble (and we should be). However, every now and then, you need to remind yourself (and others) that you really are an amazingly dope young woman.

Issa Rae delivered one of my favorite quotes of all time, when asked on the red carpet of an award show who she wanted to see win that night. "I'm rooting for everybody Black." The end. There was no uncomfortable laugh that followed, no explanation of what she meant by that, and no justification provided. She delivered that message with the straightest of faces, such that the only person uncomfortable was the interviewer. That is the level of fierceness and audacity that I wish for you. You are dope because you are. You belong. You are needed. Most importantly, you are supported. We see you and are rooting for you, sis. Go forth and thrive!

CPSIA information can be obtained
at www.ICGtesting.com
Printed in the USA
BVHW041054300820
587652BV00012B/297